Civil War and Reconstruction (1850-1877)

★★ PRESIDENTS OF THE UNITED STATES ★★

By Jody Cosson

WEIGL PUBLISHERS INC.

PRESIDENTS OF THE UNITED STATES

Published by Weigl Publishers Inc.
350 5th Avenue, Suite 3304 PMB 6G
New York, NY 10118-0069
Website: www.weigl.com

Library of Congress Cataloging-in-Publication Data

Cosson, Jody.
  Civil War and Reconstruction / Jody Cosson.
     p. cm. -- (Presidents of the United States)
  Includes bibliographical references and index.
  ISBN 978-1-59036-743-8 (hard cover : alk. paper) -- ISBN 978-1-59036-744-5 (soft cover : alk. paper)
  1. Presidents--United States--Biography--Juvenile literature. 2. Presidents--United States--History--19th century--Juvenile literature. 3. United States--History--Civil War, 1861-1865--Juvenile literature. 4. Reconstruction (U.S. history, 1865-1877)--Juvenile literature. 5. United States--Politics and government--1861-1865--Juvenile literature. 6. United States--Politics and government--1865-1877--Juvenile literature. I. Title.
  E176.1.C794 2008
  973'.09'9--dc22

                    2007012645

Printed in the United States of America
1 2 3 4 5 6 7 8 9 0 11 10 09 08 07

Project Coordinator
Heather C. Hudak

Design
Terry Paulhus

Photo Credits
Every reasonable effort has been made to trace ownership and to obtain permission to reprint copyright material. The publishers would be pleased to have any errors or omissions brought to their attention so that they may be corrected in subsequent printings.

All of the Internet URLs given in the book were valid at the time of publication. However, due to the dynamic nature of the Internet, some addresses may have changed, or sites may have ceased to exist since publication. While the author and publisher regret any inconvenience this may cause readers, no responsibility for any such changes can be accepted by either the author or the publisher.

Contents

United States Presidents

REVOLUTION AND THE NEW NATION (1750–EARLY 1800s)

 George Washington
(1789–1797)

 John Adams
(1797–1801)

 Thomas Jefferson
(1801–1809)

 James Madison
(1809–1817)

 James Monroe
(1817–1825)

EXPANSION AND REFORM (EARLY 1800s–1861)

 John Quincy Adams
(1825–1829)

 Andrew Jackson
(1829–1837)

 Martin Van Buren
(1837–1841)

 William Henry Harrison
(1841)

 John Tyler
(1841–1845)

 James Polk
(1845–1849)

 Zachary Taylor
(1849–1850)

 Millard Fillmore
(1850–1853)

 Franklin Pierce
(1853–1857)

 James Buchanan
(1857–1861)

CIVIL WAR AND RECONSTRUCTION (1850–1877)

 Abraham Lincoln
(1861–1865)

 Andrew Johnson
(1865–1869)

 Ulysses S. Grant
(1869–1877)

DEVELOPMENT OF THE INDUSTRIAL UNITED STATES (1870–1900)

 Rutherford B. Hayes
(1877–1881)

 James Garfield
(1881)

 Chester Arthur
(1881–1885)

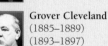 **Grover Cleveland**
(1885–1889)
(1893–1897)

 Benjamin Harrison
(1889–1893)

 William McKinley
(1897–1901)

THE EMERGENCE OF MODERN AMERICA (1890–1930)

 Theodore Roosevelt
(1901–1909)

 William H. Taft
(1909–1913)

 Woodrow Wilson
(1913–1921)

 Warren Harding
(1921–1923)

 Calvin Coolidge
(1923–1929)

THE GREAT DEPRESSION AND WORLD WAR II (1929–1945)

 Herbert Hoover
(1929–1933)

 Franklin D. Roosevelt
(1933–1945)

POST-WAR UNITED STATES (1945–EARLY 1970s)

 Harry S. Truman
(1945–1953)

 Dwight Eisenhower
(1953–1961)

 John F. Kennedy
(1961–1963)

 Lyndon Johnson
(1963–1969)

CONTEMPORARY UNITED STATES (1968 TO THE PRESENT)

 Richard Nixon
(1969–1974)

 Gerald Ford
(1974–1977)

 Jimmy Carter
(1977–1981)

 Ronald Reagan
(1981–1989)

 George H. W. Bush
(1989–1993)

 William J. Clinton
(1993–2001)

 George W. Bush
(2001–)

A Country Divided

The North and the South fought the Civil War from 1861 to 1865.

"I look upon it [the Civil War]…as a war of sentiment and opinion by one form of society against another form of society."

James Mason, Virginia Senator

As the 1860s approached, the United States was being torn apart. Railroads and water travel had united the country, but something greater had divided it. Americans shared a language, most of their beliefs, and pride in their country, but the issue of slavery had come between the North and the South.

Since 1619, slaves had helped tame U.S. land. Even the country's leaders had owned slaves. Southern **plantations** had become dependent on slave labor, but most northerners thought it was morally wrong to own another human being.

The Missouri Compromise of 1820 drew an imaginary line between the North and the South. It outlawed slavery in the **territories** North of that line. The Kansas-Nebraska Act of 1854 repealed the Missouri Compromise. It allowed slavery in the territories. This act angered many northerners. In 1858, Abraham Lincoln and Stephen Douglas **debated** about the issue of slavery, widening the rift between the North and the South.

Lincoln opposed the spread of slavery. He defeated Douglas in the 1860 presidential election. Before Lincoln could take office in 1861, South Carolina had **seceded** from, or left, the United States. Six other states followed shortly after. These seven states formed the Confederate States of America, otherwise known as the Confederacy.

The Union and the Confederacy could not agree on who owned southern military forts. In April of 1861, Confederate troops took Fort Sumter in South Carolina by force, starting the Civil War. Shortly after, Lincoln called for Union volunteers to fight the Confederacy. This act prompted four more states to secede from the Union and join the Confederacy. In the end, the North fought to end slavery, and the South fought to keep it.

Following the war, the country began the slow process of Reconstruction. During Reconstruction, Congress tried to help African Americans make the transition from slavery to freedom. Over the next several years, **amendments** were added to the **Constitution**. These amendments outlawed slavery, made former slaves citizens, and gave African American men the right to vote.

The later part of the 19th century is often called the Gilded Age. The Gilded Age was named for a book written by Mark Twain and Charles Dudley Warner that discussed the practices of some of the country's leaders. Some of these people had became rich through corrupt and dishonest business deals. During the Gilded Age, the United States became a modern, industrialized nation. The economy thrived with the production of manufactured goods. Immigrants poured into the country. With new railroads, transportation of people and goods became easier than ever.

Abraham Lincoln's Early Years

Abraham Lincoln was born on February 12, 1809, on a farm in Kentucky. His family lived in a one-room log cabin on the frontier. When Abraham was two years of age, the family moved to a larger farm.

At seven years of age, Abraham and his family moved to Indiana. They lived in a lean-to shed until a log cabin was built. The land they owned was in a forest. Young Abraham worked hard, chopping down trees to clear the forest for farmland.

The year 1818 was a difficult one for Abraham and his family. Abraham was kicked hard in the head by a horse. He recovered, but later that year, his mother died from drinking poisoned milk.

A year later, Abraham's father remarried a widow with three children. Abraham and his stepmother got along well. She encouraged him in his studies. He and his older sister attended school off and on. Abraham later figured that he probably attended one complete year of school. His parents could not read or write.

> "…Of course when I came of age I did not know much. Still somehow, I could read, write, and cipher…but that was all."
>
> *Abraham Lincoln*

Abraham Lincoln's mother, Nancy Hanks Lincoln, died when Abraham was nine years old.

Lincoln helped his father and neighbors with plowing and planting, but he never liked physical labor. He loved to read. He spent his spare time reading the family Bible and other books he was able to borrow from neighbors.

When Lincoln was 19, he and a friend took a flatboat loaded with farm produce down the Mississippi River to New Orleans. In 1830, he moved to Illinois with his family. He split rails and helped cleared his father's farmland, but he did not stay long. The next year, he left on another boat trip to New Orleans.

When he came home, Lincoln decided to strike out on his own. He left his family and moved to New Salem, Illinois. He clerked in a general store, helped out at the mill, and did odd jobs. In his free time, he educated himself by reading.

Lincoln quickly made friends in New Salem. His friends and neighbors encouraged him to run for the Illinois **legislature**. He was only 23 years old, but they though Lincoln would do well in government.

The general store where Lincoln worked was failing. He needed money, so he joined the state militia and went to serve in the Black Hawk War. The Black Hawk War was an effort to move American Indians out of Illinois. Lincoln was elected by his company to serve as their captain. This brought him great pride and happiness. Although he never saw battle, serving in the militia taught Lincoln how to be a leader, and it gave him the confidence that he needed to succeed as a politician.

Lincoln served three months in the state militia. By the time he got home from the war, he had little time to **campaign** for the election. Lincoln was unable to get enough votes to be elected, but he was not going to give up. He had received most of the votes from his community. They believed he could represent them in government.

After losing the election, Lincoln went into business with a friend. Their store soon went into debt. Lincoln was elected as postmaster of New Salem and worked as a surveyor to pay for the store. In 1835, his business partner died, leaving the rest of the debt for the store to Lincoln. It took him many years, but he was able to pay off the debt.

Lincoln headed down the Mississippi River on a flatboat when he was 19 years old.

Lincoln's Early Political Career

> **"'A house divided against itself cannot stand.' I believe this government cannot endure, permanently half slave and half free."**
>
> *Abraham Lincoln, June 16, 1858*

In 1834, Lincoln ran again for the Illinois legislature. This time he won. He was re-elected three times, serving a total of eight years. During this time, Lincoln studied law. Within two years, he earned his lawyer's license. In 1837, Lincoln helped get the Illinois state capitol moved to Springfield so it was more centrally located in the state. He moved to Springfield and began to practice law.

Lincoln slowly began to reveal his beliefs on slavery. He believed slavery was wrong, but he did not wish for it to be outlawed completely. He wanted to stop the spread of slavery to new states and territories.

During his early political career, Lincoln started a family. In 1842, he married Mary Todd. Mary was from a wealthy Kentucky family. Her family did not approve of Lincoln. Since he had grown up poor on the frontier, he had not learned correct manners and social graces. The two married anyway. They had four sons, but one of them died as a baby.

In 1846, the Whig party chose Lincoln to run for the U.S. Congress. He was elected, but his term in Congress was disappointing. He made no headway on the issue of slavery. Because of a deal he made with his party, Lincoln did not run for re-election.

Lincoln returned to Springfield in 1849. He threw himself into his law career. He was successful and became well-known throughout the state. Lincoln

Lincoln and his wife, Mary, had three sons. They were Robert, William, and Thomas.

Abraham Lincoln debated with Stephen Douglas over the issue of slavery in a series of debates across Illinois in 1858.

had almost forgotten about politics, but in 1854, he became shocked by what was going on in government.

Congress had passed the Kansas-Nebraska Act put forth by Stephen Douglas, a Democratic senator from Illinois. This act repealed the Missouri Compromise of 1820, which outlawed slavery north of Missouri. The Kansas-Nebraska Act allowed new states to choose whether to allow slavery or not. Douglas called this freedom of choice "popular sovereignty." The passing of this act angered Lincoln and many other northerners. He was once again elected to the Illinois legislature. He soon resigned this seat to bid for the U.S. Senate, but he could not get the bid, and another candidate was elected.

In the mid 1850s, the Whig party began to divide. Lincoln joined a new branch that called themselves the Republicans. He ran for the U.S. Senate in 1858 as a Republican against his rival, Stephen Douglas. In the late summer and fall of 1858, Lincoln and Douglas held a series of debates on slavery in towns across Illinois. Thousands of people came to listen to these debates. Douglas won the U.S. Senate election in November, but Lincoln had received important exposure. Illinois, and even parts of the nation, now knew Lincoln and what he stood for.

THE RISE OF THE REPUBLICAN PARTY

The newly formed Republican party rose out of the increasing debate over slavery. The Republicans wanted to stop the spread of slavery. The party ran its first presidential candidate in 1856, but was unsuccessful. In 1860, the country was divided, and so were politics. Several small parties were formed, each with its own ideas about how to solve the issue of slavery. The main party, the Democrats, were divided on slavery. The Northern Democrats and the Southern Democrats each had a candidate for president. Another party, the Constitutional Union, had a candidate. With the Democrats divided, and other votes going to a fourth candidate, the Republican party was able to secure the election. Today, the two main political parties in the United States are the Republicans and Democrats.

Lincoln's Presidency and the Start of the Civil War

> "I have no purpose, directly or indirectly, to interfere with the institution of slavery in the states where it exists." *Abraham Lincoln, first Inaugural Address, March 4, 1861*

In 1860, Lincoln made his bid for the presidency. In order to run for president, he had to get the Republican Party's support. The person to be supported by the party was chosen at the Republican National **Convention**. Lincoln was not the favorite to begin with, but after several rounds of voting, he was chosen as the Republican presidential candidate. In the election of 1860, Lincoln defeated Stephen Douglas and two other candidates to win the election. The son of a poor frontier farmer would be president of the United States.

Southerners were angry that Lincoln had been elected. They knew his government would threaten their way of life. They did not want the federal government telling them what to do. Southern Democrats wanted state governments to have more power. They felt each state should be allowed to do what it wanted in regards to slavery and other matters. Lincoln believed that a strong country needed a strong central government. If the Union was to survive, the states needed to come together under one common government.

Just six weeks after the election, South Carolina seceded from the United States. By the time Lincoln took office on March 4, 1861, six more states had seceded. These states formed a new country and called themselves the Confederate States of America, or the Confederacy. They elected Jefferson Davis, a senator from Mississippi, as their president.

Jefferson Davis became president of the Confederate States of America in 1861.

The Confederacy took over U.S. land and buildings within their boundaries. Fort Sumter in South Carolina was under siege. Lincoln was unsure of what to do. If he sent troops, South Carolina would think Lincoln wanted a war. If he removed U.S. troops from the fort, he would acknowledge South Carolina as belonging to a new country. Meanwhile, supplies at the fort were running low. Lincoln decided not to send troops, but he sent ships with supplies. When the ships arrived on April 12, 1861, the Confederate Army fired on Fort Sumter. Three days later, Lincoln called for 75,000 volunteers who were to be used as soldiers for the Union Army. The country was at war. Lincoln's call for troops caused four more states to secede and join the Confederacy.

The slave states of Maryland, Missouri, Kentucky, and Delaware remained with the Union. These were called border states. While these states never officially seceded from the Union, Confederate supporters there caused some

problems, such as rioting. Lincoln was forced to send troops into Maryland and Missouri to calm the people and arrest troublemakers.

The first Civil War battle, the Battle of Bull Run, was fought in Virginia, in July 1861. The Union Army planned to win the battle, march on to take the Confederate Capitol of Richmond, and end the war. The North soon found out it would be much more difficult to defeat the South. Confederate troops were able to make the Union army retreat, winning the battle. Lincoln was shocked at the loss of life on the battlefield. He quickly replaced his general of the Army of the Potomac with General George McClellan. In November 1861, Lincoln made McClellan general-in-chief of all Union forces.

The violence of the Battle of Bull Run shocked the American people and the government.

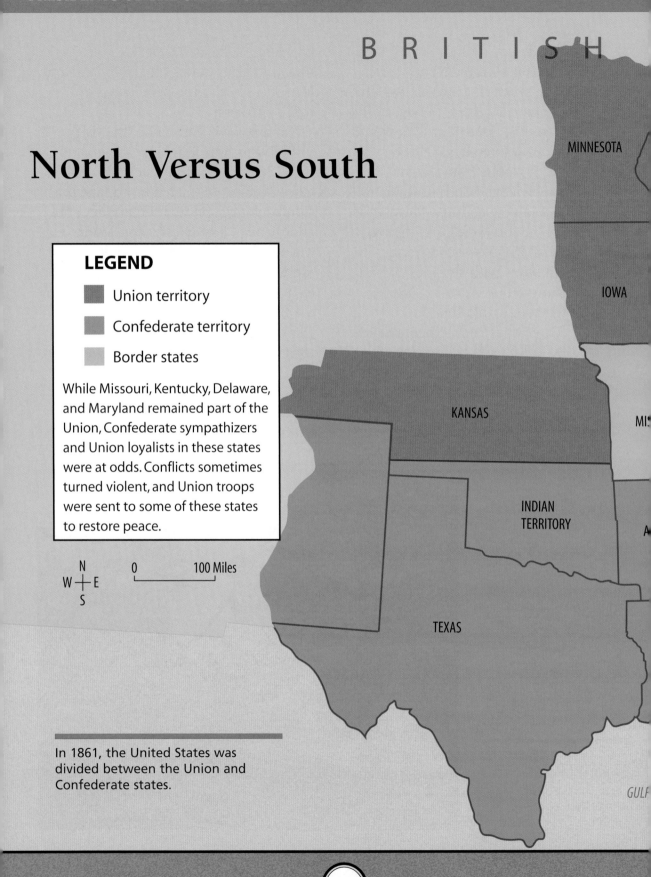

North Versus South

LEGEND

- Union territory
- Confederate territory
- Border states

While Missouri, Kentucky, Delaware, and Maryland remained part of the Union, Confederate sympathizers and Union loyalists in these states were at odds. Conflicts sometimes turned violent, and Union troops were sent to some of these states to restore peace.

N
W—E
S

0   100 Miles

In 1861, the United States was divided between the Union and Confederate states.

BRITISH

MINNESOTA

IOWA

KANSAS

MI

INDIAN
TERRITORY

A

TEXAS

GULF

A M E R I C A

LAKE SUPERIOR

CANADA

LAKE HURON

MAINE

...SCONSIN

LAKE ONTARIO

NEW
HAMPSHIRE

LAKE MICHIGAN

NEW YORK

VERMONT

MICHIGAN

MASSACHUSETTS

LAKE ERIE

RHODE ISLAND

PENNSYLVANIA

CONNECTICUT

ILLINOIS

OHIO

NEW JERSEY

INDIANA

DELAWARE

VIRGINIA

MARYLAND

KENTUCKY

NORTH
CAROLINA

TENNESSEE

SOUTH
CAROLINA

MISSISSIPPI

ALABAMA

GEORGIA

...ANA

ATLANTIC OCEAN

FLORIDA

Lincoln as the Great Emancipator

B y early 1862, it appeared as if the Confederacy was winning the war. Confederate generals, such as Robert E. Lee and Thomas "Stonewall" Jackson, were more aggressive and experienced than Union generals like McClellan.

As Lincoln dealt with hardship in the war, tragedy struck at home. In February 1862, the Lincolns' son, William, became sick and died. "Willie" as his parents called him, was only 11 years old. The Lincoln's were devastated by the death of Willie. Mary went into a deep depression, but Lincoln could not let his grief overcome him. He needed to stay strong for the Union.

Lincoln's political view of slavery was that he wanted to contain it to states where it was already legal. His main goal was preserving the Union. His personal view, however, was that all men, regardless of race, should be free. By mid-1862, he believed he could free the slaves, while gaining the upper hand in the war. Upon advice from his cabinet, Lincoln waited until the Union Army had a victory to present his ideas.

Lincoln was the author of the Emancipation Proclamation.

This victory came in September 1862, at the Battle of Antietam. On September 22, Lincoln presented a draft of the **Emancipation** Proclamation to Congress. The final draft was put into effect on January 1, 1863. The Emancipation Proclamation stated that all slaves in the Confederacy were free. Lincoln did not want to anger the border states by freeing their slaves. Doing so, he thought, might cause them to secede.

At first, the Emancipation Proclamation did not have much effect on slavery. Since the Confederacy no longer considered themselves part of the United States, they did not have to follow U.S. laws. There was no way Lincoln could enforce the proclamation. The Emancipation Proclamation did have political impact. The outcome of the war would decide whether slavery would continue or be abolished in the United States.

In summer 1863, the Union had two important victories. One was at Gettysburg, Pennsylvania. After three days of fighting, and a combined 50,000 casualties on both sides, Confederate General Lee was forced to retreat. Meanwhile, Union General Ulysses S. Grant led his troops to capture Vicksburg, Mississippi. This battle gave the Union control of the Mississippi River, which divided the Confederacy in two.

In November 1863, Lincoln traveled to Gettysburg to dedicate the Gettysburg National Cemetery. There, he delivered one of his most famous speeches, the Gettysburg Address. In his speech, Lincoln honored the soldiers who fought and died there.

THE GETTYSBURG ADDRESS

Lincoln was not the main speaker at the dedication of Gettysburg National Cemetery. Edward Everett, a well-known speaker, spoke for two hours before Lincoln. Lincoln's speech was 272 words long. It lasted only two minutes. After Everett's long speech, the crowd expected Lincoln's speech to last longer. When it ended quickly, they clapped politely. Lincoln felt his speech was a failure. Little did he know how famous and revered his speech would become. It became known as the Gettysburg Address and is probably the most recognized speech in American history.

"Four score and seven years ago our fathers brought forth on this continent, a new nation, conceived in Liberty, and dedicated to the proposition that all men are created equal."

"Now we are engaged in a great civil war, testing whether that nation, or any nation so conceived and so dedicated, can long endure. We are met on a great battle-field of that war. We have come to dedicate a portion of that field, as a final resting place for those who here gave their lives that the nation might live. It is altogether fitting and proper that we should do this."

"But, in a larger sense, we can not dedicate—we can not consecrate—we can not hallow—this ground. The brave men, living and dead, who struggled here, have consecrated it, far above our poor power to add or detract. The world will little note, nor long remember what we say here, but it can never forget what they did here. It is for us the living, rather, to be dedicated here to the unfinished work which they who fought here have thus far so nobly advanced. It is rather for us to be here dedicated to the great task remaining before us—that from these honored dead we take increased devotion to that cause for which they gave the last full measure of devotion—that we here highly resolve that these dead shall not have died in vain—that this nation, under God, shall have a new birth of freedom—and that government of the people, by the people, for the people, shall not perish from the earth."

Lincoln's Second Term and the End of the Civil War

Abraham Lincoln was re-elected to serve another term as president in 1864.

Lincoln had removed McClellan from his post as general-in-chief shortly after the Battle of Antietam. McClellan had failed to follow General Lee when Lee retreated back to Confederate territory. Lincoln was upset that McClellan had not finished the battle, which could have ended the war. Lincoln appointed several more generals who were no more successful than McClellan. In March 1864, he named General Ulysses S. Grant as general-in-chief. Grant's plan was to wear down the Confederate Army. His plan worked. Large Southern cities, such as Mobile, Alabama, and Atlanta and Savannah, Georgia, were surrendering.

In 1864, Lincoln ran for a second term as president. General George McClellan ran against him, saying he would end the war. People had grown tired of the war but they were encouraged by the recent Union victories. Lincoln was re-elected.

Congress had put forth an amendment of the constitution to abolish slavery in the

"…With malice toward none, with charity for all, with firmness in the right as God gives us to see the right, let us strive on to finish the work we are in, to bind up the nation's wounds…to do all which may achieve and cherish a just and lasting peace among ourselves and with all nations."

Abraham Lincoln, second Inaugural Address, March 4, 1865

entire Union. Lincoln used his influence to gain support for the amendment. Congress passed the 13th Amendment to the Constitution on January 31, 1865. Before it could be made into law, three-fourths of the states needed to formally approve it.

By the beginning of 1865, the South was in rough shape. Union troops had burned their cities, their houses and barns, and their crops. People were going hungry. Thousands of slaves had escaped to the North, and many Confederate soldiers had deserted the army. Knowing the end was near, Jefferson Davis tried negotiating peace with President Lincoln. No agreement was reached because Lincoln required that the Confederacy surrender completely.

In April 1865, General Grant's forces broke through the last line of Richmond's defense. Nothing was standing between them and the capitol of the Confederacy. As Union troops marched on, Confederate troops and government officials fled Richmond. They set fire to parts of the city as they left. The Union took control of the Confederate capitol. Lincoln came to Richmond a few days later to see the city's defeat for himself. He was able to walk into Jefferson Davis' study and sit in his chair.

On April 9, 1865, General Lee surrendered to General Grant at Appomattox Courthouse, Virginia. The war was over.

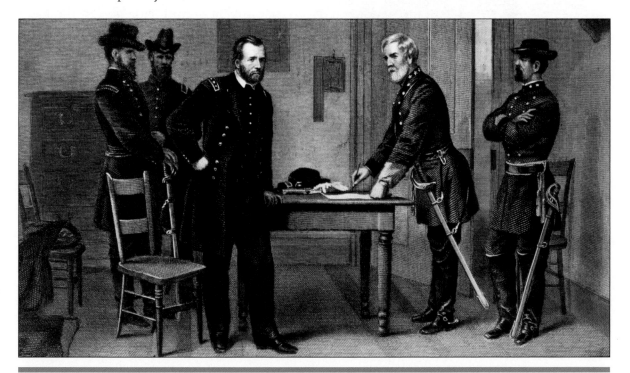

Confederate General Robert E. Lee surrendered to Union General Ulysses S. Grant at Appomattox Courthouse, Virginia.

Lincoln's Assassination and Legacy

The Civil War was over, and the Union had won. President Lincoln was looking forward to the reconstruction of the South and welcoming these states back into the Union. He had accomplished his goal of preserving the United States of America.

After the war, soldiers from the North and the South went home. In the South, many slaves learned that they were free. They rejoiced. The country celebrated. Then the country grieved. The man who had led the United States through its worst crisis was dead.

Just five days after Lee's surrender to Grant, President Lincoln and his wife went to see a play. They sat in a box near the stage in Ford's Theater in Washington, D.C. An actor named John Wilkes Booth was at the theater that night. Booth was a Confederate sympathizer. He

blamed President Lincoln and his administration for the country's troubles. During the play, Booth entered the box Lincoln was in and shot him in the back of the head. Lincoln was carried to a house across the street. His family and friends waited anxiously to see whether Lincoln would live or die. At 7:22 a.m. on April 15, 1865, President Lincoln died. The man who had fought so hard to hold the country together was gone.

The country mourned President Lincoln. Thousands of people gathered at the capitol to pay their respects to the fallen president. When Lincoln's body was sent home to Springfield for burial, crowds gathered around his casket. People now looked to Vice President Andrew Johnson to unify the country.

John Wilkes Booth shot President Lincoln at Ford's Theater on April 14, 1865. Lincoln died the next morning.

While trying to keep the country together, President Lincoln welcomed two new states to the Union. Before the Civil War, Virginia was much larger than it is today. The people in Western Virginia wanted to remain in the Union. On June 20, 1863, West Virginia became a separate state. Nevada had just become a territory at the beginning of the Civil War. On October 31, 1864, Nevada became the 36th state.

While most presidents came from wealthy backgrounds, Lincoln had been a frontier farmer, a rail-splitter, and a failed storekeeper. He had little formal education. His advisors had downplayed his skill as a courtroom lawyer. They said he was a "common man." Lincoln became president of a divided country. Many people doubted that this man from the backwoods of Illinois could unite the nation.

Lincoln may have had a common upbringing, but he was not a common man. He made some of the hardest decisions imaginable to preserve his country. Lincoln did what no one

thought could be done. He led the nation to peace and freedom for all. Lincoln, along with George Washington, is known as one of the greatest presidents of the United States.

THE LINCOLN MEMORIAL

The Lincoln Memorial stands at one end of the National Mall in Washington, D.C. Its 36 columns represent the 36 states in the Union when Lincoln was president. A huge statue of Lincoln sits looking down over the reflection pond in front of the memorial. The Gettysburg Address and Lincoln's second Inaugural Address are carved into its walls. The Lincoln Memorial honors the man who led the United States through the most terrible turmoil in American history to peace and freedom for all.

Thousands of people watched Lincoln's funeral procession in Washington, D.C.

Andrew Johnson's Early Years

Andrew Johnson was born in a log cabin in Raleigh, North Carolina, on December 29, 1808. His father died when Andrew was three years old. His mother worked as a laundress and a weaver to support her two sons. She remarried, but the family was still very poor.

> "The state which I represent …took me by the hand, and that generous, that brave, that patriotic people, have made me all that I am…"
>
> *Andrew Johnson*

Andrew Johnson became the 17th president of the United States.

Andrew and his brother became apprentices to a tailor. In return, they were given food and lodging. While Andrew and the other apprentices sewed, frequent customers would sometimes read aloud to them. Andrew had never been to school, but he was given a book, and he taught himself to read.

In 1826, Johnson and his family moved to Greeneville, Tennessee. There, Johnson set up his own tailor shop. Soon after, he met Eliza McCardle. Eliza was the daughter of the village shoemaker. The two married in 1827. Eliza had been educated, and while Andrew worked in his shop, Eliza read to him. She taught him grammar, spelling, writing, and mathematics. Over the course of their long marriage, the Johnsons had three sons and two daughters.

In 1830, Johnson was elected the mayor of Greeneville. He found that he liked politics. Johnson thought of himself as a common man, and he connected with working-class people. The people in town and nearby counties liked to hear his down-to-earth speeches.

Over the next 35 years, Johnson would hold almost every type of political office. He was elected to the state legislature in 1834 and was re-elected in 1838. After serving those terms, he was elected to the state senate.

From 1843 to 1853, Johnson served as a Democrat in the U.S. House of Representatives. He was elected governor of Tennessee and served from 1853 to 1857. As governor, Johnson worked to provide public schooling for the children of Tennessee. As part of this effort, he established a state library.

From 1857 to 1862, Johnson served as a U.S. Senator. Johnson's political views sometimes contradicted each other. He approved of slavery and owned slaves, but he hated rich plantation owners. As a Southern Democrat, Johnson favored strong state governments with more rights, but he supported the preservation of the Union.

When the Civil War began, Johnson tried unsuccessfully to keep Tennessee in the Union. He was the only Southern senator who did not leave the U.S. Senate. In March 1862, Lincoln named Johnson the military governor of Tennessee. Johnson strongly supported Lincoln's goal of keeping the country united.

Johnson supported Lincoln's ideals and ran as his vice president.

Johnson's Vice Presidency, Presidency, and Reconstruction

Abraham Lincoln chose Johnson, a Democrat, as his vice president in the 1864 election. Johnson was chosen to attract Democrats to the Union cause and to reward them for their loyalty to the Union. Lincoln was re-elected, and Johnson was made vice-president. Johnson would be vice-president for only 42 days before taking over for the **assassinated** President Lincoln.

Johnson could have easily met the same fate as President Lincoln. In a conspiracy plot to destroy Lincoln and his cabinet, an associate of John Wilkes Booth was sent to assassinate Johnson the same night that Lincoln was assassinated. The man never made the attempt, and Johnson became president.

Reconstruction was Johnson's first order of business. Like Lincoln, Johnson believed that the Southern states should be restored to the United States. At first, Johnson had Confederate leaders and wealthy plantation owners arrested. Soon, he began to let them go, or pardon them, as long as they took an oath of allegiance to the Union. He began allowing former Confederate states back into the Union. Once 10 percent of a states' voters of European ancestry made an oath of allegiance to the Union, they were allowed to elect state governments. They would be re-admitted to the union after drafting a state constitution recognizing the 13th Amendment, which abolished slavery.

Andrew Johnson took the oath of office after the assassination of President Lincoln.

In his plan for Reconstruction, Johnson failed to protect the newly freed slaves. Since he believed in states' rights, he thought each state should decide what to do with the former slaves, called freedmen. Johnson had pardoned Confederate leaders and wealthy plantation owners, so these men were free to run for state and national offices. The new southern state legislatures did not seem much different from the old ones. They passed "Black Codes," which allowed people of European ancestry to keep their control over the freedmen. The Black Codes did not allow freedmen the right to arm themselves. They could not hold large meetings. Freedmen who were unemployed could be arrested and hired out to employers. Some states only allowed freedmen to do the kinds of jobs slaves had done.

Johnson went ahead with his plan for Reconstruction before Congress was in session. He declared Reconstruction over at the end of 1865. The mostly Republican Congress thought Johnson had been too easy on the South. They were angry that Johnson refused to protect the freedmen. They were furious that these decisions were made without their consent. Congress would have a much different plan for Reconstruction.

"I must be permitted to say that I have been almost overwhelmed by the announcement of the sad event which has so recently occurred. I feel incompetent to perform duties so important and responsible as those which have been so unexpectedly thrown upon me."
Andrew Johnson, April 15, 1865

President Johnson implemented his plan for Reconstruction before Congress was in session.

Johnson and Congress

When they came into session in December 1865, Congress formed the Joint Committee of Reconstruction. In February 1866, Congress voted to give more power to the Freedmen's Bureau, a program that helped protect former slaves. Johnson vetoed this bill because it would override the state courts. He did not feel that it was the state governments' job to protect freedmen. Congress secured enough votes to pass this bill anyway. A few months later, Congress passed the Civil Rights Act of 1866. This act made freedmen U.S. citizens and gave them equal rights under law. Johnson vetoed this bill and viewed it as an invasion of states' rights. Congress was able to pass the act anyway. Congress passed the 14th Amendment, which was similar to the Civil Rights Act, but gave African American men the right to vote. Johnson did not agree with the amendment, and the South refused to **ratify** it. It became obvious that President Johnson and the Republicans in Congress could not seem to agree.

During the 1866 campaign for Congress, Johnson went on a disastrous speaking tour called the "Swing around the circle." He spoke in support of Democratic congressional candidates that held his views, and he spoke strongly against his Republican Congress. His efforts hurt his cause more than they helped. Hecklers lured him into raging shouting matches. Fights broke out in the crowds.

Crowds of people celebrated outside the U.S. House of Representatives when Congress passed the Civil Rights Act of 1866.

Johnson's campaign had the opposite effect that he wanted. Radical Republicans won most of the seats in Congress. The Congress became even more hostile towards Johnson. They took over Reconstruction efforts and passed acts to make him powerless to stop them.

In early 1867, Congress passed the Tenure of Office Act. The act stated that the president had to get Senate approval before he could dismiss any government official. This included members of the president's cabinet. In the summer of 1867, when Congress was not in session, Johnson suspended Secretary of War Edwin M. Stanton. Stanton was working with the Republicans against Johnson's efforts at Reconstruction. President Johnson appointed General Ulysses S. Grant to replace Stanton. When Congress reconvened, it refused to agree with Stanton's suspension. General Grant returned the office to Stanton, but President Johnson dismissed Stanton again, replacing him with a new secretary of war. Because of this act, Congress began **impeachment** proceedings against President Johnson.

Congress passed the Army Appropriations Act. This act removed the president's right to command the army. Both this act and the Tenure of Office Act were in violation of the Constitution and were eventually repealed.

Secretary of War Edwin M. Stanton was suspended by President Johnson in 1867. This action led to Johnson's impeachment trial.

RECONSTRUCTION ACTS OF 1867

The Reconstruction Acts of 1867 put the former Confederacy under a state of military rule. With the exception of Tennessee, the Southern states were divided into five military districts, each ruled by a Union general. Each district had to register all adult male voters. Each district had to elect a convention to prepare a state constitution. The state constitution had to give African American males the right to vote. If the voters accepted the constitution, a state government could be set up. Next, the state legislature had to accept the 14th Amendment. If Congress approved the state constitution, the state might be readmitted to the Union. By mid-1870, all of the states had followed these steps and were readmitted to the Union.

Impeachment

The U.S. Constitution allows for the president, vice president, and other officers of the U.S. government to be impeached. Impeachment can occur due to treason, bribery, or other big or small crimes.

The U.S. Senate tries the impeachment. The Chief Justice presides over the impeachment trial. Two-thirds of the Senate members must vote in favor of impeachment in order for the president to be impeached.

Impeachment includes removal from office. The person who is impeached cannot hold any U.S. office ever again. If the person is found guilty of a crime, that person can be tried in a court of law. The court of law will decide the punishment of the impeached person.

On February 24, 1868, the U.S. House of Representatives approved a resolution to impeach President Andrew Johnson. The final vote was 126 to 47. A committee of seven radical Republicans was created to report articles of impeachment. Johnson was charged with eight counts of violating the Tenure of Office Act, two counts of libeling Congress, and one count of violating the Command of the Army Act. Part of the committee believed that Johnson had conspired to have Lincoln assassinated. They wanted to charge Johnson with involvement in the assassination, but that charge was withdrawn.

The impeachment trial began in the Senate on March 30, 1868. Johnson was not present during the trial. Five lawyers defended him. At first, the public was so interested in this trial that gallery passes were given out. These passes allowed the public to watch the trial proceedings.

On May 16, the Senate voted on the 11th and last

Tickets were sold to Johnson's impeachment trial.

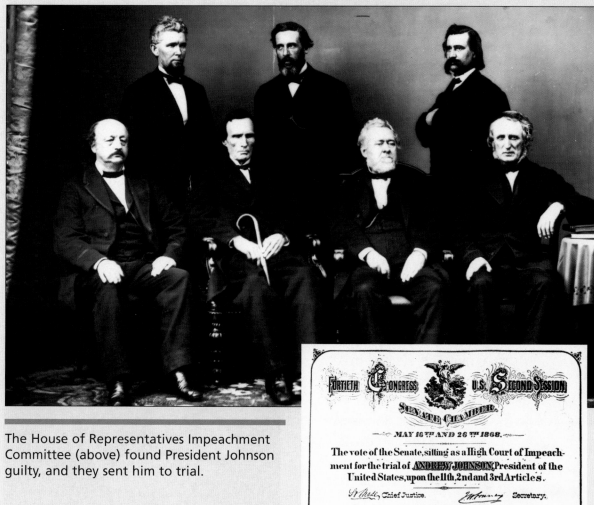

The House of Representatives Impeachment Committee (above) found President Johnson guilty, and they sent him to trial.

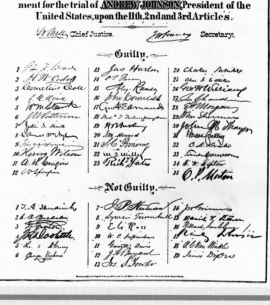

Article of Impeachment. This article included many of the charges in the other articles. The Senate was one vote short of the two-thirds majority needed to impeach the president. On May 26, another vote was taken on the 2nd and 3rd Articles of Impeachment, but the two-thirds majority vote was not reached. The president was found not guilty.

The Senate was one vote short, and Johnson was not impeached.

Johnson's Later Years and Legacy

After being found not guilty, Johnson served the rest of his term as president. He and Congress continued to disagree on Reconstruction efforts. Johnson vetoed Congress' bills on Reconstruction, and Congress would override his vetoes. In this way, Congress continued to implement their plan of Reconstruction during the few remaining months of Johnson's presidency. By July 28, 1868, enough states had ratified the 14th Amendment, and it was added to the Constitution.

Johnson's near impeachment ended his hopes for re-election. The Democrats would not **nominate** him for re-election. They chose Horacio Seymour to run against the Republican General Ulysses S. Grant. Grant was elected in November 1868.

After leaving the White House, Johnson and his family returned to Greeneville, Tennessee. For a few years, he tried unsuccessfully to get elected to the U.S. Congress. In 1874, he was elected as a U.S. Senator. Johnson was the only president to become a U.S. Senator after his term in office. On March 20, 1875, Johnson delivered his last speech, still attacking the Republicans. He died on July 31, 1875.

After leaving office, Johnson served as a U.S. Senator.

Andrew Johnson became president during one of the most difficult times in American history. The Civil War had ended, but the country was still divided. Johnson had the opportunity to unify the nation, but at a time when the country needed to come together, the government was fighting itself. Never before had Congress and the president been so at odds.

Johnson's policies on slavery were contradictory. He had owned slaves but had supported the freeing of slaves and the end of slavery. Johnson did not protect the people he had helped set free, and he tried to stand in the way of a government who would protect them.

Although he was found not guilty, Johnson will always be remembered as the first president to be tried for impeachment. He has been called one of the worst presidents in U.S. history.

> "I intend to devote the remainder of my life to the vindication of my own character." *Andrew Johnson*

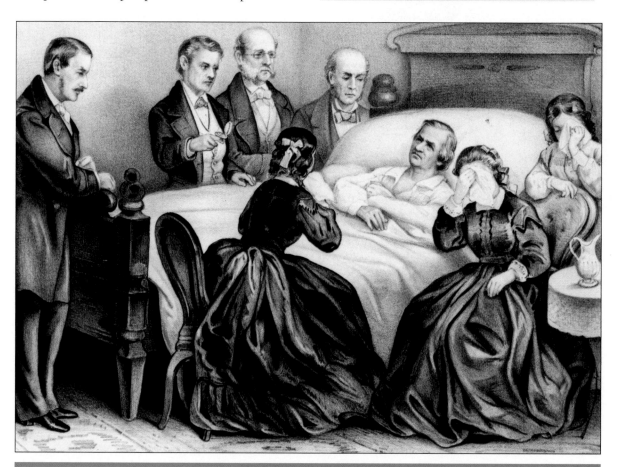

Doctors and family members surrounded Andrew Johnson on his deathbed.

Ulysses S. Grant's Early Years

Hiram Ulysses Grant was born in Point Pleasant, Ohio, on April 27, 1822. His father was a leather tanner. Hiram, known as "Ulysses" to his friends and family, was the oldest of six children. His two brothers went into the tannery business, but Ulysses wanted nothing to do with it. He preferred to spend his time with horses. At a young age, he rode and drove horses and took over the plowing of the family land. Ulysses did these chores while attending school full time.

Ulysses' father valued education. He managed to get Ulysses an appointment to the U.S. Military Academy at West Point. The congressman who secured Ulysses' appointment signed his name as Ulysses Simpson Grant. The name stuck. Grant attended West Point from 1839 to 1843. He graduated in the middle of his class.

After graduating, Grant met his West Point roommate's sister, Julia Dent. Julia was from a wealthy St. Louis family. Grant and Julia were engaged for four years, and they married in 1848. They had three sons and one daughter.

In 1845, Grant's regiment was sent to Texas. Both the United States and Mexico claimed land in southern Texas. War broke out

Ulysses S. Grant, a Civil War hero, became the 18th president of the United States.

"In answer to your letter of a few days ago asking what 'S' stands for in my name I can only state nothing. It was a mistake made…when application was first made…to West Point…After I received my Diploma and Commission, with the 'S' inserted…and have so signed my name ever since." *Ulysses S. Grant*

shortly after the United States annexed Texas. Although Grant did not approve of the Mexican-American War, he fought hard. He was rewarded with the temporary rank of first lieutenant and captain.

Grant's regiment was sent to the West Coast in 1852. He had to leave his family behind. His wife was expecting their second child, who was born while Grant was away. Grant was unhappy in California. He missed his family, and he wanted to see his new son. After two years, he resigned from the army and returned to St. Louis.

In St. Louis, Julia's family gave Grant a piece of land to farm. Grant was not a good farmer, and his crops failed. He sold firewood on street corners in St. Louis. He tried real estate, but was unsuccessful. Grant was desperate to provide a living for his family. Even so, Grant freed the one slave he owned.

In 1860, Grant moved his family to Galena, Illinois, and worked in his father's leather store. He was unhappy there. During his time in Galena, he paid close attention to the intense debate on slavery and states' rights.

Ulysses S. Grant and his wife, Julia, were married in 1848.

General Grant and the Civil War

When the Civil War broke out between the North and the South, Grant quickly volunteered to lead a regiment of troops for the Union. Grant was appointed colonel and given an Illinois volunteer regiment. He led his men to fight Confederate sympathizers in Missouri.

In February 1862, Grant's regiment attacked Fort Henry and Fort Donelson in Tennessee. The Confederates surrendered both forts. The Confederate commander was a friend of Grant's. He asked for a truce and terms of surrender, thinking Grant would go easy on him. Grant demanded "unconditional and immediate surrender." The Confederate commander surrendered, and people nicknamed Grant "Unconditional Surrender Grant." The Union had their first major victory. Grant became famous overnight.

In April 1861, Grant and his troops fought at the Battle of Shiloh. Surprised by Confederate troops, Grant's men were barely able to hold them off. They were saved only when another Union army arrived to help them fight. The battle had been a disaster. Grant was removed from his command over the Army of Tennessee. That October, President Lincoln changed his mind, saying "I cannot spare this man. He fights." Grant regained control of the Army of Tennessee and became commander of Union forces in the West.

In the spring and summer of 1863, Grant led his men on a siege of Vicksburg, Mississippi. The siege lasted six weeks before Vicksburg surrendered. The surrender allowed the Union forces to take control of the Mississippi River, dividing the Confederacy in two.

Despite difficulties at the Battle of Shiloh, General Grant became commander of the Union army.

Grant was appointed general-in-chief of the Union Army by President Lincoln in March 1864. Unlike generals before him, Grant was bold and assertive. He began a campaign of total warfare, constantly trying to engage Confederate troops and wear them down. This plan worked. Over the next few months, the Confederate Army dwindled to half the size of the Union Army. General Grant became a national hero. He even received votes for the presidential nomination at the 1864 Republican Convention.

In June 1864, Union and Confederate troops met at Petersburg, Virginia. Unable to take the city right away, Grant and his men settled down for an extended siege. This siege lasted through the winter and into early April 1865. Meanwhile, under Grant's direction, General William Tecumseh Sherman led his troops on a march through Georgia. They burned everything in their path and captured Atlanta and Savannah. When Grant's forces were able to break through Petersburg, they had a clear path to Richmond, Virginia, the Confederate capital. Grant's troops marched on, arriving in Richmond on April 3, 1865. They found Richmond burning. The Confederate government had fled.

General Lee surrendered to General Grant on April 9, 1865, at Appomattox Courthouse, Virginia. Grant offered General Lee and his men generous terms of surrender. He allowed Confederate troops to keep their horses and mules. He fed them and told them they could go home. The Civil War was over.

> "I felt like anything rather than rejoicing at the downfall of a foe who had fought so long and valiantly, and had suffered so much for a cause, though that cause was, I believe, one of the worst for which a people ever fought, and one for which there was the least excuse."
>
> *Ulysses S. Grant*

ROBERT E. LEE

General Robert E. Lee was the Confederate counterpart to General Grant. When the Civil War began, President Lincoln offered Lee the command of the Union troops. Lee had to decide between the United States and his native Virginia. When Virginia seceded from the Union, Lee chose Virginia. He joined the Confederate army and was eventually named commander in chief of all Confederate armies.

General Lee is considered a military genius. His brilliant military strategy was the only thing that upheld the Confederacy against the larger, stronger Union Army. His aggressive strategy engaged Union troops, often defeating them.

When the war ended, Lee took defeat nobly. He surrendered to Grant in full military dress and thanked him for his generous terms of surrender.

Grant's Rise to the Presidency

John Wilkes Booth was supposed to kill two men the night he shot President Lincoln. His second target was Grant. General Grant should have been at the same play Lincoln attended, but he decided not to go. This decision saved his life.

During Andrew Johnson's presidency, Grant was appointed as full general of the armies of the United States. Johnson sent Grant on a tour of the South. Grant reported his thoughts on Reconstruction to the president. In August 1866, Grant went on a speaking tour with President Johnson. Johnson's crude speeches and angry outbursts made Grant lose respect for him.

In 1867, Grant served for a short time as secretary of war under President Johnson. When Congress insisted that Edwin M. Stanton be reappointed, Grant resigned. Grant later supported the impeachment of President Johnson.

In May 1868, the Republicans unanimously nominated Grant for president. Grant ended his nomination acceptance letter with, "Let us have peace." This became the slogan of his campaign. Grant easily won the election of 1868 and became the 18th president of the United States.

Although he had been a great leader on the battlefield, Grant was not a good president. He had never served in office before and did not know very much about how the government worked. He chose his friends as advisors, unconcerned about how knowledgeable they were. Many times, they were unqualified and failed in their positions.

In the 1868 election, the Republican Party supported Grant for president and Schuyler Colfax for vice president.

In 1869, Grant signed an Act to Strengthen the Public Credit. It pledged that the government would buy back paper money that had been issued during the war. Since gold was worth more than the paper money, the government would buy it back with gold at a reduced price.

Jay Gould and Jim Fisk wanted to get rich quick. They bought as much gold as they could. They used Grant's brother-in-law, Abel Rathbone Corbin, to try to keep Grant from selling gold, which would make the price drop. Grant did not realize that they were using him in their scheme. When he found out, Grant ordered the sale of government gold. Gold prices plummeted, and the U.S. gold market collapsed. Many people lost money, and President Grant was partly to blame.

On March 30, 1870, the 15th Amendment was officially ratified. The amendment guaranteed all citizens the right to vote. On this date, he also welcomed Texas back into the United States. Texas was the last state to be re-admitted to the Union.

Although the Southern states had agreed to allow African American men to vote, they did not protect that right. In the South, groups such as the Ku Klux Klan harmed African Americans for trying to vote or run for office.

In May 1870, the first of three Enforcement Acts was put in place to ensure African Americans the right to vote. In the first act, Congress made it a federal crime to interfere with a person's right to vote. It stated that the federal government could take action against interference when a state government would not. Grant used federal troops in South Carolina to protect African American voters from the Ku Klux Klan.

In February 1871, Congress passed the second act that said the federal government would supervise all elections in cities larger than 20,000 people. The third act, passed in April 1871, outlawed the use of wearing disguises and threatening people. This act was passed specifically to stop the Ku Klux Klan.

"The responsibilities of the position I feel, but accept them without fear. The office has come to me unsought; I commence its duties untrammeled. I bring to it a conscious desire and determination to fill it to the best of my ability to the satisfaction of the people."
Ulysses S. Grant, March 4, 1869

KU KLUX KLAN

The Ku Klux Klan, a Southern hate group, began in Pulaski, Tennessee, soon after the end of the Civil War. At first, the Klan was to be a social club for ex-Confederates, but the group's purpose quickly changed. The Ku Klux Klan did not think African Americans should have the same rights as they did. The Klan rebelled against Reconstruction and sometimes resorted to violence towards African Americans and people who sided with them.

Grant's Foreign Policy and Second Term

Grant relied heavily on Hamilton Fish, his secretary of state, for foreign policy. Fish was one of the few good appointments Grant had made. Against Fish's advice, Grant made plans to annex Santo Domingo, which is now the Dominican Republic. Grant wanted to use the island as a naval base. He also thought it would be a good place for freed slaves to relocate. He proposed a treaty to the Senate, but the Senate rejected the treaty.

During the Civil War, Confederate ships were built and supplied by Great Britain. The building of these ships violated Great Britain's neutrality. Great Britain supplied other arms to the Confederates during the war. The United States wanted damages for the violation of neutrality and support of the Confederacy. An international court settled U.S. claims against Great Britain. This was called the Treaty of Washington. The court awarded $15 million to the United States.

"The acquisition of Santo Domingo is desirable because of its geographical position. It commands the entrance to the Caribbean Sea and the Isthmus transit of commerce…. Its possession by us will in a few years build up a coastwise commerce of immense magnitude, which will go far toward restoring to us our lost Merchant Marine. It will give to us those articles which we consume so largely and do not produce, thus equalizing our imports and exports."

Ulysses S. Grant

Some of the **liberal** Republicans were unhappy with Grant. They felt that he allowed too much corruption in government and business. These people combined with the Democrats and nominated Horace Greely for president. The Republican party nominated Grant to run for president again in 1872. Grant won the election and began his second term. Grant's second term was filled with even more **scandal**. Although Grant was not a part of the corruption, his friends and government officials were.

In 1872, it was discovered that some government officials, including Grant's vice president, Schuyler Colfax, created a fake company to do construction work for the railroads.

This company charged the government millions of dollars, and the money was pocketed by government officials. Other schemes, including dishonest tax collection and fraud by government officials, damaged President Grant's reputation as well.

In the early 1870s, railroads were booming. New railroad construction led to more than 35,000 miles of tracks. Banks were investing in these new railroads. One bank, called Jay Cooke and Company, was one of the largest investors. In September 1873, Jay Cooke and Company realized that they had overextended themselves financially. They went bankrupt. This sent the country into a panic. Other banks and businesses closed. Investors sold their stocks, damaging the economy further. The New York Stock Exchange suspended trading for 10 days to stop the stock market from going any lower. This was known as the Panic of 1873. This panic led to a five-year depression. By 1876, more than 14 percent of the U.S. workforce was unemployed.

Grant was unable to ease the country's financial burden. He refused to release paper money back into the economy. He was afraid that more money would lead to inflation, which would make the money worth less.

By 1874, the country had lost faith in the Republican government and its president. The 1874 elections led to the Democrats controlling the House of Representatives. Although Reconstruction would not formally be over until 1877,

the Democratic control of Congress stalled any further Reconstruction, and even repealed some of the existing laws.

Corruption in his administration was a heavy load for Grant to carry.

FIRST LADY JULIA GRANT

Julia Grant loved being First Lady. She felt the position of First Lady should hold more dignity and social standing. She set out to accomplish this by holding fancy dinner parties and teas. She welcomed people of all social levels to the White House. Her greatest feat was the wedding of her daughter Nellie. It is still known as one of the most lavish affairs to ever take place at the White House. Julia wept when she left the White House. Later, she remembered her time there as the best years of her life.

The Whiskey Ring

During Grant's presidency, the country was expanding west. Railroads were carrying goods and people all over the country. Industry was booming, and there was money to be made. This era was called the Gilded Age. President Grant's friends and family were involved in dishonest schemes to get rich. One of the biggest schemes was the Whiskey Ring.

Lincoln's administration had imposed high taxes on whiskey to help pay for the Civil War. The whiskey tax was used to pay war debts and help pay for Reconstruction. Republicans formed the Whiskey Ring in 1871 to raise funds for political campaigns in Missouri and other western states. The ring made money by selling more whiskey than it reported to the Treasury Department. The money went toward Republican campaigns and to newspapers that printed favorable stories about the Grant administration.

Once Grant was re-elected, the ring no longer needed money for campaigns. The whiskey money then went to ring members. By 1873, the Whiskey Ring had defrauded the Treasury Department of $1.5 million. Secretary of the Treasury Benjamin H. Bristow suspected that the treasury was being defrauded, but he needed to prove it. By 1875, he had the evidence he needed. In May 1875, the Treasury Department seized whiskey operations in St. Louis, Chicago, and Milwaukee.

This political cartoon shows Grant as a trapeze artist trying to hold up his corrupt administration.

Orville E. Babcock, Grant's private secretary, was involved in the Whiskey Ring. Babcock and Grant had been close friends since the Civil War. People thought that if the president's private secretary was involved, the president might also be involved.

As a politician, President Grant was almost blindly loyal to his friends. Babcock denied his involvement in the ring. Grant believed him, even though the evidence pointed to his guilt. Grant testified on Babcock's behalf at his trial. Because the president testified for him, Babcock was found not guilty.

"Let no guilty man escape unless it can be avoided."

Ulysses S. Grant, in a note to Bristow in July 1875

Orville E. Babcock, Grant's private secretary, was involved in the Whiskey Ring. Babcock was found not guilty because of President Grant's testimony.

Grant's Later Years and Legacy

Grant's supporters wanted him to run for a third term, but Grant had no plans to run. The Republicans would not nominate him. After a highly contested election, Rutherford B. Hayes became president on March 3, 1877. Grant retired from the White House.

In May 1877, Grant and his family began a trip around the world. They toured Europe, the Middle East, and Asia. The family was well

received almost everywhere they went. Grant was honored, not as a former president, but as a Civil War hero. People in the United States read of their travels in newspapers. The Grant family remained a popular part of American culture. The Grants returned to America on December 16, 1879.

In 1880, Grant was placed for nomination on the Republican ticket; however, he did not receive the nomination. James A. Garfield was nominated and won the election. In August 1881, Grant and his family moved to New York City. He invested in a business partnership with a man who swindled him out of all of his money.

After a long military and political career, Grant faced financial difficulties in retirement.

Grant was bankrupt. When an article he wrote about the Battle of Shiloh sold well, he decided to write his **memoirs** to make money for his family.

In 1884, Grant was diagnosed with throat cancer. He was dying, but he hurried to finish his book. Grant wrote about the Civil War and his career as a soldier. The book was a huge success, but he would not see any of the money it would make. Grant died on July 23, 1885, shortly after finishing his book.

During Grant's early years in office, Reconstruction was changing the South. The 15th Amendment became law during his presidency. It granted African American males the right to vote. He pursued and punished members of the Ku Klux Klan. At the end of his term, however, Reconstruction was dying. Democrats had taken control of Congress, and the country was too consumed by the financial crisis to continue reconstructing the South.

Although President Grant's administration was full of scandals, he was an honest man. Ulysses S. Grant would be the first to admit that he was at his best on the battlefield. Congress defeated many of the programs he championed, and he was unable to stop corruption and scandal from overrunning his administration. Grant will always be remembered for his heroic role in leading the Union to victory in the Civil War.

"I never thought of acquiring rank in the profession I was educated for; yet it came with two grades higher prefixed to the rank of General officer for me. I certainly never had either ambition or taste for political life; yet I was twice president of the United States. If any one had suggested the idea of my becoming an author, as they frequently did, I was not sure whether they were making sport of me or not. I have now written a book which is in the hands of the manufacturers."

Ulysses S. Grant, May 23, 1885

GRANT'S TOMB

Ulysses S. Grant and his wife, Julia Dent Grant, are entombed at General Grant National Memorial in New York City. The memorial is commonly called Grant's Tomb. The memorial was constructed from 1891 to 1897, and was dedicated on April 27, 1897. More than 1 million people attended the parade and dedication ceremony. The granite and marble structure is the largest tomb in North America.

Timeline

From 1850 to 1877, the United States was in turmoil. The issues of states' rights and slavery divided the nation. When the southern states seceded from the Union, Abraham Lincoln fought to keep the country together, even going to war to save the nation. Slaves were given their freedom, and the Union won the war. When Lincoln was assassinated, Andrew Johnson took over the difficult task of Reconstruction.

1850-1855	1856-1859	1860-1862	1863-1865
PRESIDENTS			
In 1854, Abraham Lincoln speaks out against the Kansas-Nebraska Act in Peoria, Illinois.	In 1858, Abraham Lincoln and Stephen Douglas hold a series of debates on slavery. 	Abraham Lincoln is elected as president in 1860.	Abraham Lincoln is assassinated on April 14, 1865. Vice President Andrew Johnson takes over as president.
UNITED STATES			
In 1854, the Kansas-Nebraska Act is passed, allowing slavery in the territories. This repeals the earlier Missouri Compromise that outlawed slavery in the territories north of Missouri.	John Brown leads a raid on Harper's Ferry in 1859, with the goal of leading a slave rebellion.	The Civil War begins in 1861 with shots fired on Fort Sumter. Eleven Southern states secede from the Union and form the Confederate States of America.	On April 9, 1865, General Robert E. Lee surrenders to General Ulysses S. Grant, ending the Civil War.
WORLD			
The Crimean War is fought between Russia on one side and the Ottoman Empire, Great Britain, France, and Sardinia on the other side.	The Franco-Austrian War is fought in 1859 to free Italy of Austrian rule.	Moldavia and Wallachia unite to form Romania in 1861.	The Taiping Rebellion ends in China. More than 20 million Chinese people die in the rebellion.

Johnson and Congress could not come to an agreement about Reconstruction, and this led to Johnson's near impeachment. Congress took over Reconstruction, passing amendments guaranteeing equal rights and the right to vote for African American men. Ulysses S. Grant was brilliant on the battlefield but ineffective as a president. Grant's corrupt administration reflected poorly on him. Grant re-admitted the last of the southern states into the United States, and tried to protect the voting rights of African Americans. When the Democrats took over Congress, Reconstruction declined and ended a short time later.

1866-1869	1870-1872	1873-1877
PRESIDENTS		
President Andrew Johnson's impeachment trial begins March 30, 1868. He is later found not guilty and serves the rest of his term.	Ulysses S. Grant is re-elected to his second term as president in 1872.	In 1875, President Grant testifies on behalf of Orville E. Babcock, his private secretary, who is involved in the Whiskey Ring.
UNITED STATES		
The 14th Amendment makes former slaves U.S. citizens.	Texas is the last state to be re-admitted into the United States after it ratifies the 15th Amendment that gives all men the right to vote, regardless of race.	Jay Cooke and Company goes bankrupt, setting off the Panic of 1873.
WORLD		
The United States purchases Alaska from Russia in 1867.	From 1870 to 1871, the Franco-German War is fought between France and Germany.	From 1877 to 1878, the Russo-Turkish War is fought between Russia and Turkey.

Activity

A debate is an argument with rules. Presidential candidates often hold debates to let voters know their positions on different issues. Lincoln and Douglas debated the issue of slavery, among other things. Debating is an important skill. It teaches people how to research a topic in a thoughtful way. Debating is a good way to learn how to express a specific point of view.

1. Choose a debate partner who will take the opposite side of the issue.

2. Study this book and other sources to learn more about Reconstruction. Make notes, and think of several arguments to promote your viewpoint. You could write each argument on a note card.

3. Practice reading your notes in private.

4. When you are ready to hold the debate, have another person time your speech. Each side gets two minutes to make a statement. Each statement should take the opposite viewpoint of the preceding statement from the other side. Try not to repeat ideas until you are ready to make your final summary statement.

Pro-2 minutes maximum
Con-2 minutes maximum
Pro-2 minutes maximum
Con-2 minutes maximum

Continue until all statements have been made.

5. Each side gives a final summary statement of its position.

Quiz

1. True or False? Abraham Lincoln was the first Republican president.

2. How did Andrew Johnson become president?
   A. The Republicans voted for him.
   B. The Democrats voted for him.
   C. He was vice president when Lincoln was assassinated.

3. True or False? The Emancipation Proclamation freed all of the slaves.

4. How many states seceded from the United States to form the Confederate States of America?
   A. 8   B. 11   C. 15

5. Who was supposed to be with President Lincoln the night he was assassinated?
   A. Ulysses S. Grant
   B. Andrew Johnson
   C. Stephen Douglas

6. True or False? The result of an impeachment trial could mean the president has to leave office.

7. What state was the last to be re-admitted to the United States?
   A. Alabama
   B. Texas
   C. South Carolina

8. What was the Gilded Age?
   A. Industry boomed, and some people made fortunes.
   B. Slaves were freed.
   C. People went to California to hunt for gold.

9. True or False? Grant served three terms as president.

Answers 1. True 2. C 3. False. The proclamation only freed slaves in the Confederate states. 4. B 5. A 6. True 7. B 8. A 9. False. Grant only served two terms.

Further Research

Books

To find out more about U.S. presidents, visit your local library. Most libraries have computers that connect to a database for researching information. If you enter a keyword, you will be provided with a list of books in the library that contain information on that topic. Non-fiction books are arranged numerically, using their call number. Fiction books are organized alphabetically by the author's last name.

Websites

The World Wide Web is also a good source of information. Reputable websites usually include government sites, educational sites, and online encyclopedias. Visit the following sites to learn more about U.S. presidents.

The official White House website offers a short history of the U.S. presidency, along with biographical sketches and portraits of all the presidents to date. **www.whitehouse.gov/history/presidents**

This website contains background information, election results, cabinet members, and notable events for each of the presidents. **www.ipl.org/div/potus**

Explore the lives and careers of every U.S. president on the PBS website. **www.pbs.org/wgbh/amex/presidents**

Glossary

amendments: additions to a bill or constitution that improve it

assassinated: the violent killing of a political leader

campaign: a series of events and speeches with the goal of getting a candidate elected to office

constitution: a document that outlines the laws that govern a country or state

convention: a meeting of members of a political party to elect candidates for office

debated: argued or discussed a topic

emancipation: to set free

impeachment: to question a person's conduct

legislature: official body of elected officials who make laws

liberal: favoring reforms that extend democracy and freedom and distribute wealth more evenly

memoirs: someone's account of his or her life

nominate: to suggest someone to run for a political office

plantations: large southern farms where crops, such as tobacco or cotton, are grown

ratify: to formally confirm or approve something

scandal: an event that causes public outrage

seceded: withdrew from a group or union

territories: areas of land that belong to a country, such as the United States, but are not states

Index